THIS BOOK IS
DEDICATED TO ALL THE
CHILDREN AROUND THE WORLD.

TO ENCOURAGE
THEM TO DREAM BIG
AND TO NEVER STOP LEARNING.

The Alphabet that Changed the World is a not for profit project that came together through the collaboration of 26 inspiring artists from all around the globe.

The goal with this alphabet book is to create more awareness and understanding of each other's cultures and encourage conversations at home with your children that will allow them to grow with a more in-depth understanding of the world and its many complexities. **100%** of the profits from this book will be donated to charity.

The global conversation around racism is moving at lightning speed, and whilst we have made our fair share of mistakes, we are all doing our best to keep up - but we don't just want to keep up, we want to create change. We want to do our part in advancing the discussion and creating awareness around race and culture to positively impact the world around us.

Each artist was given a letter and asked to select someone they believed has had a positive influence on society and would provide a great cultural learning experience for children and parents alike. The artists had free choice to complete the artwork in a way that best represented them and their unique artistic style.

"Read more, learn more, change the globe" - NAS

THE ALPHABET THAT CHANGED THE WORLD.

Any reference contained in this book to public figures or their works does not constitute or imply the endorsement, recommendation or approval of those people

Aa

is for

Muhammad Ali

"If my mind can conceive it,
and my heart can believe it,
then I can achieve it"

Artwork by Gavin Morrison

Bb

is for

Barack Obama

"Our destiny is not written for us, but by us"

Artwork by Alex Lehours

Cc

is for

Cathy Freeman

"You got to try and reach for the stars,
or try and achieve the unreachable"

Artwork by Na'Tarlia Costell Doyle

Dd

is for

Princess Diana

"Life is just a journey"

Artwork by Ches Longdy

Ee

is for

Elaine Brown

"Our freedom is tied to the freedom of everyone"

Artwork by Jordan Ellington Marble

Ff

is for

Frida Kahlo

"I am my own muse. I am the subject I know best. The subject I want to know better"

Artwork by Cici Chon

Gg

is for

God

"Greater is He that is in me than he that is in the world"

Artwork by Victoria Gabriel

Hh

is for

Jim Henson

"The most sophisticated people I know-
inside they are all children"

Artwork by Meri Biscotto

Ii

is for

Ida B Wells

"The way to right wrongs is to shine the light of truth upon them"

Artwork by Chloe McAlister

Jj

is for

Julio Cortázar

"All profound distraction opens certain doors. You have to allow yourself to be distracted when you are unable to concentrate"

Artwork by Mylène Dosal

Kk

is for

Colin Kaepernick

"And he took a knee so that justice would be for all"

Artwork by Maurice Jackson

Ll

is for

Bruce Lee

"Always be yourself, express yourself, have faith in yourself"

Artwork by Janie de Guzman

Mm

is for

Martin Luther King Jr

"I have a dream"

Artwork by Sem Sokly

Nn

is for

Albert Namatjira

"I must look after and care for my father's country. It is important that my family and I look after a place like this"

Artwork by Kayla Bowen

is for

Oprah Winfrey

"Turn your wounds into wisdom"

Artwork by Samantha Knightbridge

Pp

is for

Pablo Picasso

"Every child is an artist. The problem is how to remain an artist once they grow up"

Artwork by Antoine Donte

Qq

is for

Queen Nefertiti

"A person can accomplish anything and rule their own world, regardless of gender, race and religion. Everyone needs to walk tall and empower each other"

Artwork by Camille Lambie-Knight

Rr

is for

Sir Kenneth Robinson

"To be creative you actually have to do something"

Artwork by Shawn Huddleston

Ss

is for

Steve Jobs

"The only way to do great work is love what you do"

Artwork by Mat Hede

Tt

is for

Mother Teresa

"Peace begins with a smile"

Artwork by Rico Rose

Uu

is for

Tana Umaga

"That's the way - giving heart and soul in everything you do! We're not playing Tiddleywinks here"

Artwork by Shannah Mae Gibson

Ww

is for

Walt Disney

"All of our dreams can come true,
if we have the courage to pursue them"

Artwork by Scott Brinkley

Xx

is for

Malcolm X

"Education is the passport to the future"

Artwork by Vanessa Ursina Segovia

Yy

is for

Malala Yousafzai

"One child, one teacher, one book, one pen can change the world"

Artwork by Rajiv Fernandez

Zz

is for

Ziggy Marley

"Love is a chance we take and the answer forever"

Artwork by Emily Vriesman

Meet The Artists...

B is for Barack Obama

ALEX LEHOURS @alexlehours

Nickname:
Lehours

Favourite Song:
Hotel California - The Eagles

If I could change one thing in the world it would be...
Common courtesy. A very easy and manageable fix without asking too muc[h] each other. I feel a lot would change and benefit in the world if we all becam[e] a bit more courteous toward one another. These days it feels as if everyone seems their time and place is more valuable than others. It has become a ve[ry] self absorbed existence and I would love if we could all step back and consid[er] others around us more often.

P is for Pablo Picasso

ANTOINE DONTE @antoinedonte

Favourite Song:
Off The Wall - Michael Jackson

If I could change one thing in the world it would be...
To stop all racism.

Q is for Queen Nefertiti

CAMILLE LAMBIE-KNIGHT @missclk_

Nickname:
Cammy

Favourite Song:
Me, myself and I - Queen B

If I could change one thing in the world it would be...
To make everyone love themselves unconditionally.

I is for Ida B Wells

CHLOE MCALISTER @chloemcalister_

Favourite Song:
That's like choosing a favorite child! Anything by Placebo or Deftones.

If I could change one thing in the world it would be...
"That would be harsher punishment for parole violators, Stan." - Miss Congeniality.

F is for Frida Kahlo

CICI CHON @craftycici

Nickname:
Cici

Favourite Song:
Such a hard question because I love so many artis[ts] such as The Beatles, Prince, Queen, The Cranberries, Kendrick Lamar, Chanc[e] the Rapper, Jack Johnson, and Michael Jackson... But I will say that Dreams by The Cranberries has a special place in my heart because it was our wedding theme song :-)

If I could change one thing in the world it would be...
To end homelessness.

Z is for Ziggy Marley

EMILY VRIESMAN @emilyvpcreates

Favourite Song:
New Light - John Mayer

If I could change one thing in the world it would be...
...make sure all children felt represented. Through books they read, through positive role models in the media and in their lives, and through open, inclusive people in society around them. A child should be embraced fully—no matter their ethnicity, the language they speak, the pronunciation of their name, their gender, or their lifestyle.

A is for Muhammad Ali

GAVIN MORRISON @lefthands2you

Nickname:
Esky

Favourite Song:
Santa Monica - Everclear

If I could change one thing in the world it would be...
To see people visit or communicate without the use of social pipes. Just put the device down and actually see the person instead of a screen (don't get me wrong I like social media lol).

L is for Bruce Li

JANIE DE GUZMAN @janie.de.guzman

Nickname:
J.J.

Favourite Song:
Wouldn't It Be Nice - The Beach Boys

If I could change one thing in the world it would be...
...a more open mind to different cultures, ethnicites, and lifestyles. We should love each other because at the end of the day, we are all human and we owe that to each other.

V is for Dorothy Vaughan

JAY CORPREW @artandgalaxies

Nickname:
Jay

Favourite Song:
Somewhere Over The Rainbow/What a Wonderful World performed by Israël Kamakawiwo'ole.

If I could change one thing in the world it would be...
To end humanities ability to hate or harm one another.

E is for Elaine Brown

JORDAN ELLINGTON MARBLE @jemarble

Nickname:
JEM

Favourite Song:
Last Call - Kanye West

If I could change one thing in the world it would be...
...would have free healthcare and education for everyone.

N is for Albert Namatjira

KAYLA BOWEN

Favourite Song:
Breakdown - Ar'mon and Trey

If I could change one thing in the world it would be...
That all children grow up safe and happy.

S is for Steve Jobs

MAT HEDE @takeheed

Favourite Song:
Dont Stop Me Now - Queen

If I could change one thing in the world it would be...
Free education for all.

K is for Colin Kaepernick

MAURICE JACKSON JR @cp21v

Nickname:
Reese

Favourite Song:
Knocks Me off My Feet - Stevie Wonder

If I could change one thing in the world it would be...
To change the cost of living or the hourly minimum wage to a much higher amount.

H is for Jim Henson

MERI BISCOTTO @augusteight.create

Nickname:
Mez

Favourite Song:
Blood on the Leaves - Kanye West

If I could change one thing in the world it would be...
Attitudes. Specifically the level of understanding, appreciation and communication between people. I would put more focus on play, interaction and communication to help strengthen our interactions with humans, nature and animals. We all have our part to play and our own stories to tells and there's a lot we could learn from each other if we shifted our focus and attitudes.

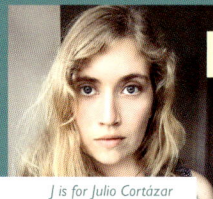
J is for Julio Cortázar

MYLENE DOSAL @studiomylene

Nickname:
Myl

Favourite Song:
Sing by Travis - The Invisible Band

If I could change one thing in the world it would be...
To see a world in which education and books are available to everyone.

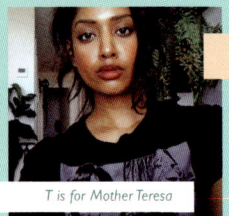
T is for Mother Teresa

RICO ROSE @ricoroseart

Nickname:
Rico

Favourite Song:
One Love - Bob Marley

If I could change one thing in the world it would be...
Global warming.

Y is for Malala Yousafzai

RAJIV FERNANDEZ @lil.icon

Nickname:
Lil' Icon

Favourite Song:
Yeah! - Usher

If I could change one thing in the world it would be...
That the only connotation of guns and arms be my biceps.

O is for Oprah Winfrey

SAMANTHA KNIGHTBRIDGE @artbysamy

Nickname:
Samy

Favourite Song:
Video - India.Arie

If I could change one thing in the world it would be...
That every child was born into equal opportunity. Where it's not possible for a child to be less privileged or nurtured than the other. Where every kid had a chance.

W is for Walt Disney

SCOTT BRINKLEY @sbrinkley79

Nickname:
Scottie 2 Hottie

Favourite Song:
Walk - Foo Fighters

If I could change one thing in the world it would be...
That people would see each other as people. Not for their color, or past, or accomplishments, rich, poor or anything in between. But as people all just trying to make it in this world.

U is for Tana Umaga

SHANNAH MAE GIBSON @shannahmaegibson

Nickname:
Shan Shan

Favourite Song:
7 Days - Craig David

If I could change one thing in the world it would be...
To create a world where there was zero animal cruelty. And three day weekends.

R is for Sir Kenneth Robinson

SHAWN HUDDLESTON @crak703

Favourite Song:
Sardines - Junkyard Band

If I could change one thing in the world it would be...
To reprioritize quality of life to the top of the list.

X is for Malcolm X

VANESSA SEGOVIA @vanessaursinasegovia

Favourite Song:
Ms. Fat Booty - Mos Def

If I could change one thing in the world it would be...
Find equality. Imagine the amazing differences in the world if everyone's voice carried the same weight

G is for God

VICTORIA GABRIEL @victoriagabrielart

Nickname:
Queen Victoria

Favourite Song:
Nobody Greater - Vashawn Mitchell

If I could change one thing in the world it would be...
The dominant existence of Poverty, it's increasing rate and the lack of support individuals give toward eradicating it.